THE GERMAN A
ON SCARBORC

December 16 1914

"The shells which shattered the buildings of Scarborough have made no impression on the spirits of the people. Nothing could be more praiseworthy than the manner in which the town passed through its ordeal and returned to its normal life. The people of Yorkshire are proverbially hard to impress, and the stranger who came into Scarborough in ignorance would have nothing but broken buildings to tell him that this quiet seaside town had been subject to an experience unknown to an English town . . . Scarborough accepts its risks."

The Times, London

REMEMBER SCARBOROUGH!

ENLIST NOW

PUBLISHED BY THE PARLIAMENTARY RECRUITING COMMITTEE LONDON. POSTER No 41.   PRINTED BY DAVID ALLEN & SONS LD. HARROW, MIDDLESEX & ENGLAND

1   Remember Scarborough ! An oil painting by E Kemp-Welch painted immediately after the bombardment made a dramatic recruiting poster.

THE GERMAN ATTACK
ON
SCARBOROUGH

December 16 1914

Edited by
James Hartington Jones

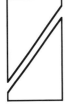
Quoin Publishing

First published 1989 by Quoin Publishing

The Barn

36a North Road

Huddersfield

West Yorkshire

Text and arrangement © Copyright Quoin Publishing
1989

ISBN 1 85563 000 1

Printed by Gorenjski Tisk, Kranj

ACKNOWLEDGEMENTS

My thanks go to the staff at the County Library in Scarborough for their assistance, access to and photocopies of material in the Scarborough Room, especially the fascinating scrapbook compiled by Mr C J T Taylor shortly after the attack. Also to staff at the Rotunda Museum and *Scarborough Evening News*. I am particularly grateful to Colin Spink of the Collectors' Centre, 34 St. Nicholas Cliff, Scarborough who allowed me to browse through his personal postcard collection and from which a number of these images are drawn. Pictures numbered 22 and 25 are from the Mary Evans Picture Library, London. Others are from my own collection.

There have been a few books previously written about the events of December 16 1914 and which can be recommended for further reading: *The German Raid on Scarborough* published by E T W Dennis & Sons, Scarborough, in two different versions; *Under German Shell-Fire* by Frederick Miller, West Hartlepool, 1915; and *Remember Scarborough 1914* by David Mould, Nelson, 1978. All are, of course, now out of print but may be consulted at Yorkshire County Library.

James Hartington Jones

July 1989

2   Rough seas break over the pier.

INTRODUCTION

Shortly before 8 o'clock in the morning on Wednesday, December 16 1914 the lookout at the Scarborough coastguard station on Castle Hill telephoned to the wireless station behind the town: "Some strange ships are approaching from the north. I cannot make out what they are. They do not answer my signals." The next message was even more urgent in tone. "They are Germans! They are firing on us !" Then the line went dead as a shell passed through the wires.

Thus was announced what the local press was to term "Scarborough's baptism of fire", as the undefended spa town became not only the first civilian target to suffer in the First World War, but the first victim of a foreign attack since 1797 and the only one involving major loss of life since the Norman invasion in 1066.

Ever since the early days of the War, there had been widespread fears of invasion but it was clearly impossible to fortify the entire east coast of Britain. An abortive attack on Yarmouth, in which the shells fell short of the town, was launched on November 3 but Scarborough - followed by Whitby and Hartlepool later in the day of December 16 - was the first attack to draw blood in the civilian population. At the time of the raid there was not a single defensive gun located at Scarborough: the only gun in place was a an ornamental Russian 64-pounder, a relic of the Crimean War. For the German navy, Scarbo-

WASHED UP BY THE TIDE AT SCARBOROUGH.

3 Washed ashore at Scarborough ! A postcard sent shortly before the outbreak of war bears no portent of the more unwelcome visitors shortly to appear from the sea.

4   The fashionable spa resort that was Edwardian Scarborough.

rough was truly a 'soft' target which proved totally unable to retaliate in any way against the hundreds of shells pumped into her homes, hotels and public buildings.

To the amazement of a number of hardy souls swimming in the sea off the beach, there emerged out of the heavy morning mist three warships: the battlecruisers *Derrflinger* and *Von der Tann* and the smaller light cruiser *Kolberg*. Of the three, the 26,180-ton, 689-foot long *Derfflinger* was the most powerful and formidable ship, launched only in 1913 and capable of up to 27 knots. She carried an armament of eight 12 inch guns, as well as smaller guns and torpedo tubes, and carried more than 1,100 crew aboard. The 19,370-ton *Von der Tann* was an older ship (1909) but carried a lethal armament of eight 11 inch guns, twenty-six lighter guns and torpedo tubes. Together, the two ships were able to deliver a devastating bombardment on a sleepy and unsuspecting seaside town.

As the attack began, the *Kolberg* steamed south and began to lay a trail of more than 100 mines as a protective measure to guard against attack from Royal Navy ships from Harwich or the Humber. In the following weeks these mines were themselves to cause havoc to shipping off the coast.

The whole town was fired upon recklessly and indiscriminately for almost half an hour. It was estimated that around 500 shells were fired and without any regard

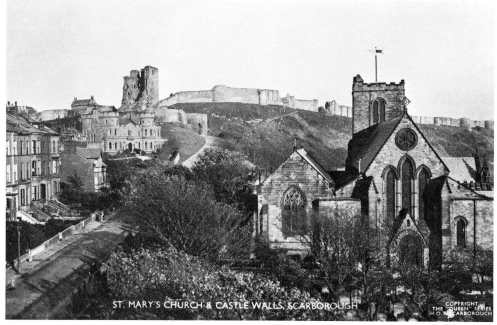

ST. MARY'S CHURCH & CASTLE WALLS, SCARBOROUGH

5   A peaceful view of St Mary's Church and the Castle.

for the horriffic civilian casualties which were caused as a result. Many of the inhabitants were at breakfast, others were still rising and some, like Alfred Beal the postman, were already going about their business. When they opened fire, the ships were reckoned to be less than half a mile offshore and most observers were initially totally incredulous at the fact that enemy ships had managed to approach so close to the town. Midway through the bombardment, when the two battlecruisers were directly opposite the Grand Hotel, an eerie silence fell as gunfire ceased for three minutes. The ordeal, however, was not over. The ships swung round and reversed their course, re-opening fire with their guns on the other side. At half-past eight, the firing ceased and and the three cruisers set course northwards at speed. In all, 17 civilians were killed - including eight women and four children, one of whom was but 14 months old - and more than 80 people were injured.

There was widespread bewilderment. There had been no instruction as to what to do in such an emergency and there were no plans for advising and controlling the populace. The civil authorities could hardly be blamed: this was, after all, the very first enemy attack on the civil population for almost a thousand years ! Many people tried to flee Scarborough, believing an invasion to be imminent. The railway station was crowded with panic stricken citizens, many still in their nightclothes, one man dressed only in a shirt and carrying a razor, another dressed in top hat and with a parrot. Extra carriages were put on departing trains to Hull, York and Leeds - any destination to escape the Hun. Motors and traps were filled

6 Pierrots performing on the crowded beach shortly before the outbreak of war. The local fishing fleet lies offshore. When the naval guns opened fire from only 600 hundred yards away, bathers in the sea fled from the beach. In the words of a contemporary account, "Naked and unashamed, surely they were not fit sport for Imperial guns !"

with women and children. A long procession of horses and carts snaked out of the town and hundreds of people simply set off on foot. Later in the day, the Post Office was besieged by residents desirous of telegraphing news of their survival to friends and relatives. The information situation was not alleviated by a ban placed on the local papers forbidding them to carry any independent accounts of the attack save for official announcements from London - which were ludicrously inaccurate and propagandist in tone. Leeds Post office declined to handle any telegrams describing the bombardment. The mayor of Scarborough was obliged to issue a notice: "I have been asked by many people what they should do in consequence of the bombardment of Scarborough this morning. I have only one piece of advice to give, and that is: 'Keep calm and help others to do the same'."

Of course, not even the authorities were completely sure of the direction in which events might turn. Troops were mobilised and 800 men of the Territorials, 8th Battalion the West Yorkshire Regiment, left York by train in the early afternoon and arrived an hour later at shell damaged Scarborough station. Crowds of residents cheered as they took up positions around the town and dug trenches on the beach in front of the Grand Hotel. Later in the afternoon, two destroyers positioned themselves off Scarborough, feeding the fears of invasion as well as reassuring the locals.

By all accounts, life returned to normal extremely quickly. Traders cleared up debris, swept up glass and dust and were opening their premises later in the morning. Places of entertainment opened that evening as normal. A brisk trade in the sale of shell fragments grew up almost immediately ! And some enterprising local photographers busied themselves selling their pictures for use as postcards: many of which are reproduced here. Over the ensuing weeks, thousands of visitors flocked to Scarborough to view the effects of the attack for themselves and the residents found themselves with an unexpected winter season on their hands.

There was to be no early revenge for the attack. The ships which had shelled Scarborough next turned their attentions to Whitby where there was a lighter 11-minute bombardment of such historic 'defensive' positions as the abbey, while the *Seydlitz, Moltke* and *Blucher* shelled the port of Hartlepool. Their brave work done, they managed to elude searching British ships, aided by fog in the North Sea, and British naval confusion caused by a serious misunderstanding of signals. Predictably, there was widespread outrage. The attack actually had the effect of firming resolve within the indignant civilian population and these fires of resentment were stoked by public figures and the press. The next day's *Daily Mirror* headline announced "German ghouls gloating over the murder of English schoolboys."

Winston Churchill, First Lord of the Admiralty, wrote to the Lord Mayor in the following terms: "Practically the whole fast cruiser force of the German Navy, including some great ships vital to their fleet and utterly irreplaceable, have been risked for the passing pleasure of killing as many English people as possible, irrrespective of sex, age or condition, in the limited time available . . . Whatever feats of arms the German Navy may hereafter perform, the stigma of the baby-killers of Scarborough will brand its officers and men while sailors sail the seas."

The Mayor was moved to observe in his reply, in much the same vein, that, "As their commanders get older in the service they will find that an iron cross pinned on their breast even by King Herod will not shield them from the shafts of shame and dishonour."

German propagandists, quite the contrary, saw the raid as a great victory discerning it as marking the end of the British navy's mastery of the high seas. The *Vienna Extrablatt* claimed on behalf of its allies: "England's presumption to rule the ocean is getting more ridiculous every day. This is one of our best victories so far." The next day's *Nurnberger Zeitung* pointed out that "For centuries their coast was secured. For decades they could rob and get rich in all corners of the world without being punished. The much smaller German fleet put the glories of England in the shade."

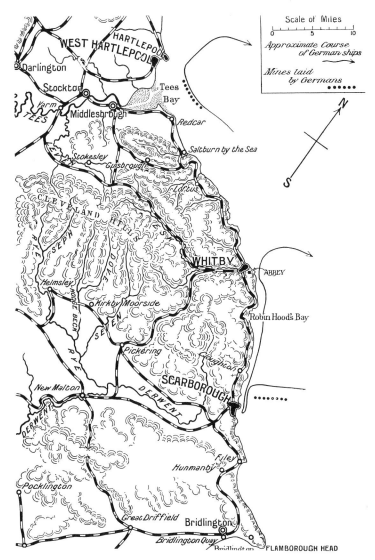

7 Map showing the the course of the German ships which bombarded the east coast towns of Scarbrough, Whitby and Hartlepool. The dotted lines indicate where the minefields were sown.

Hardly surprisingly, it was bonanza time for local recruiting offices in the north of England. Special bills and posters were printed exhorting the young and healthy to join up and wreak vengeance on the Hun and within days there were hundreds of local recruits. The powerful images of the unprovoked attack on Scarborough were to last through the whole war and the two simple words "Remember Scarborough !" became indelibly imprinted on the national consciousness. In this way, the tragedy of Scarborough directly contributed to the ultimate triumph over the German eagle.

8 Cavalry of the 14/20th King's Hussars patrolling on the sands before the attack. These cavalrymen, based at Burniston Barracks, alongwith a detachment of the Yorkshire Yeomanry, a few Territorials and a handful of Green Howards, represented the sum total of the defence force at Scarborough.

9 Lookout was kept on the east coast from fortified trenches such as these. There was little warning, however, of the German battlecruisers emerging from the mist.

10 A letter from local grocers circulated to their customers in Scarborough, August 1914. The outbreak of war brought early fears of the unknown: shortages, rationing and invasion.

SCARBOROUGH,

August 6th, 1914.

Dear Sir or Madam,

We wish to assure our friends that during the War we shall endeavour to carry on our businesses in every respect as hitherto.

We shall try to reserve our stocks entirely for our own customers, and only make such increased charges as are consistent with advancing markets. All orders will, of course, be subject to our having the goods on hand, and must be limited to moderate quantities.

The poorer section of the people cannot afford to lay in large stores of goods, and in their interests, as well as of those of the community in general, we would respectfully urge our friends to refrain from any attempt to buy in excessive quantities, and thus avoid raising of prices to an unnecessary and unreasonable figure.

To discourage the giving of orders in excess of normal requirements, our deliveries will be regulated by the supplies we have on hand, and goods will be booked out at the current price at time of delivery, not of order given.

The financial crisis arising from the War compels us to consider carefully, not only the general question of credit to all our customers, but our own position and credit as buyers on terms of cash against delivery.

Under these circumstances, and to enable us to constantly and evenly replenish stocks, we respectfully ask such of our friends as are in a position to do so to send us cash or cheques on receipt of accounts, as a steady influx of cash, with a steady replenishment of goods, will help us to keep things as near a normal level as possible—which is absolutely essential in all interests.

Panic, we should all endeavour to minimise, as the hoarding of food creates exorbitant prices in times of stress ; it should be the endeavour of everyone to avert this.

Respectfully asking for your hearty co-operation and support in our endeavours to continue our businesses at normal and reasonable prices.

We are,

Yours faithfully,

J. L. HOPWOOD,
WM. C. LAND & CO., LTD.,
JOHN ROWNTREE & SONS,
WALLIS & BLAKELEY.

11 The First Sea Lord's Room at the Admiralty in 1914. Mr Churchill,
First Lord of the Admiralty, seated at his desk, is in conversation
with Admiral of the Fleet, Lord Fisher.

Rt. Hon.
Winston S. Churchill, M.P.
First Lord of the Admiralty.

PHOTO REG HAINES.

MEN OF THE MOMENT.

12 Winston S Churchill, First
Lord of the Admiralty at the
time of the attack, depicted on a
contemporary patriotic
postcard.

13 Admiral von Hipper, the commander of the raiding force which attacked Scarborough. Dubbed "the baby-killer" in Churchill's historic attack on him, he escaped later at the Battle of Dogger Bank and was generally regarded in Germany as something of dashing naval hero.

14 Admiral Friedrich von Ingenohl. He was much criticised after the east coast raids for not maximising on the strategic opportunities which were offered that day. Tirpitz claimed, "On December 16th, Ingenohl had the fate of Germany in his hand. I boil with inward emotion whenever I think of it." Similarly, the Captain of the *Moltke*, which had shelled Hartlepool, observed that he had retreated in the face of just 11 British British destroyers "which could easily have been eliminated. Under the present leadership we will accomplish nothing." Von Ingenohl was forced to resign after the debacle at Dogger Bank the following February when the *Bluecher* was lost with almost 1,000 seamen.

15   A dramatic artist's impression - by Sam Begg of *The Illustrated London News* - of the bombardment of the south foreshore. Shells are finding their target on the Grand Restaurant.

16   Damage to the lighthouse from a shell which ricocheted off the
Grand Hotel.

GERMAN RAID, DEC.16TH 1914,
THE CASTLE WALLS, SCARBOROUGH.

17 The shell-damaged castle walls: the ten-foot thick walls were
    pierced easily by the shells in three or four places. The coastguard
    station on Castle Hill was blown to pieces. Fortuitously, the coast-
    guards had already taken refuge in the castle well.

18 Shell-damaged interior of a house at 164 North Marine Road, the
    home of Mr J H Southwick, a local postman. A shell came through
    the drawing room window, on the second floor, and destroyed fur-
    niture, mirrors and ornaments. The house next door, number 166,
    suffered similarly.

GERMAN RAID, DEC. 16TH 1914
INTERIOR OF HOUSE,
NORTH MARINE ROAD, SCARBOROUGH.

GERMAN RAID, DEC. 16TH 1914.
BACK OF ST. NICHOLAS PARADE
NEAR GRAND HOTEL, SCARBOROUGH.

19 Damage at the back of St Nicholas Parade, near to the Grand Hotel.
A shell also hit no. 17 St Nicholas Cliff, went right through the
house there and into Ashleys Boarding House in St Nicholas Parade.

GERMAN RAID, DEC. 16TH 1914.
THE GRAND RESTAURANT, FORESHORE RD, SCARBOROUGH.

20   The shattered exterior of the Grand Restaurant on the South Foreshore.

Bombardment of Scarborough by the German Fleet. Dec. 16th 1914.
The Grand Hotel.

21   The territorials arrive. Soldiers marching past the shell damaged
Grand Hotel. The Grand Hotel must have presented a large and
easy target to the German gunners. Altogether, 36 shells hit the
Hotel and restaurant, causing £10,000 worth of damage, and it
was fortunate that, the season being over, there were only two residents, who escaped unscathed.

22 Damage to the interior of the Grand Restaurant. According to the reporter from the *Daily Mirror,* all that was left intact was a decanter of wine ! Not for long one suspects !

GERMAN RAID. DEC. 16TH, 1914.
HOUSE IN LONSDALE ROAD. SCARBOROUGH

23 Another direct hit on a house at 14 Lonsdale Road. One of the first houses hit by the shelling, it was, fortuitously, empty, the occupants being away. Next door lived a well known hockey player, E Bond Railton, who had a lucky escape.

GERMAN RAID, - DEC: 16TH 1914.

HOUSE IN THE CRESCENT, SCARBOROUGH.

24 Damage to a house in The Crescent, home of the Borough Member for Scarborough, W R Rea. It was due to Mr Rea's efforts that owners of property damaged by the attack were ultimately compensated by the government. Both no. 7 and no. 8 in the elegant crescent of substantial residences were severely damaged. The occupants of no. 8 "saw the shells as they were coming like fierce balls of fire", and made their escape to the basement of the house.

25 An artist's impression, published in the *Illustrated London News*,
of German gunners aboard the battlecruisers blasting Scarbrorough
with their shells.

26 Damage at Belvoir Terrace. According to *The Scarborough Evening News*, "huge pieces of stonework were thrown about like peas" in Belvoir Terrace where three bedrooms were destroyed at no. 6 and a young woman was badly hurt.

GERMAN

DUNOLLIF, FILEY ROAD

27 A shell hit the stonework over the portal at 'Dunollie', Filey Road,
the home of Mr J H Turner, a former sheriff of Yorkshire. Another
three shells exploded in front of the house and no less than 13 at
the back ! The occupants took refuge in a boiler house at the back
of the house but a maidservant, Margaret Briggs, was killed in the
library as she went to the door to collect the letters. The local postman, Alfred Beal, died on the doorstep: he had been undeterred by
the shelling and had intrepidly carried on with the delivery of the
Royal Mail.

DEC 16TH 1914.
RBOROUGH. (2 KILLED.)

3625.   Bombardment of Scarborough, by the German Fleet. Dec: 16th 1914.
The Town Hall damaged by Shells.

29   Shells bursting over the seafront. According to the Berlin *Lokalan-zeiger*, Scarborough was "the most important harbour on the east coast of England between the Humber and the Thames." Not only a barefaced lie, but a statement which displayed some ignorance of geography !

OFFICES KINGSCLIFF CAMP, SCARBOROUGH . DEC. 16TH. 1914.

30 Soldiers on guard outside the damaged offices of Kingscliff Holi-
day Camp at 13 King Street.

GERMAN RAID, DEC 16TH 1914.
ROYAL HOTEL, SCARBOROUGH.

31 Direct hit on the Royal Hotel. An enormous hole was made in the
side of the building and every single window was broken by the
blast. Extensive damage was done to the royal suite occupied just a
short time previously by the Duke of Clarence.

WYKEHAM ST, 4 KILLED,
SCARBOROUGH BOMBARDMENT.

32 The worst casualties occurred when four people died in the rubble
    of this house at no. 2 Wykeham Street: Mrs Johanna Bennett her
    son, Albert, and two children were killed. "In this instance, the
    cruellest in a cruel catalogue, is afforded horrifying evidence of the
    German gospel of frightfulness, and their utter disregard of human
    life in their sacrifice of defenceless people," was the view taken by
    the local paper.

33　Looking into the devastated house at Wykeham Street. The surviving son, Christopher Bennett, described how he had just got out of bed and was dressing when one of the last shells came crashing through the house. "It hit the house fully and I fell through the bedroom floor, down into the kitchen. Everything fell on top of us all." They were dug out by local Territorials.

GERMAN RAID, DEC. 16TH 1914.
NO. 2. WYKEHAM STREET (4 KILLED.)

34 The scene at Wykeham Street. An eye-witness said, "The shell
    came flying straight over the railway bridge - it smashed a lot of
    windows in Gladstone Road School - and went clean through Mrs
    Bennett's house. The place was blown up."

Scarborough Local Emergency Committee.

————— ❦ —————

To Owners of Motor Cars and Bicycles.

In the event of a hostile landing all Motor Vehicles and Bicycles must be driven away at once, with or without passengers, to the Collecting Area, Hagg House, on the Pickering Road, between Thornton Dale and Pickering.

They may go by the Scalby Road or Lady Edith's Drive through Hackness, Troutsdale, and Snainton, or by Stepney Hill to Ayton, proceeding thence by the Pickering Road.

Spare tyres, spare parts, and Petrol must also be taken away, but if this is impossible, the Petrol must be run off and the Tyres, &c., rendered useless. Motor Cars and Bicycles which cannot be taken away at once must be rendered useless, but only on the distinct order to this effect from the Military Authority or the Chief Constable.

Such Order, which is in readiness, will be sent out to each Owner by a Special Messenger in the event of a landing being actual or imminent.

All enquiries in connection with the above should be addressed to Mr. Councillor White, Tranby House, Westwood, Scarborough.

35 Instructions to civilians in Scarborough following the bombardment.

37 A shell went through the roof of All Saint's Church (below) and there was also damage to the roof of St Hilda's Church (opposite).

38 The men of Yorkshire were exhorted to join up and avenge the attack. AVENGE SCARBOROUGH - UP AND AT 'EM NOW appeals were posted in all the recruiting offices. By all accounts, the local recruiting stations were besieged by applicants.

36 Wrecked shop in Prospect Road. Mrs Merryweather, wife of the proprietor, was killed at the door as **she** opened up to admit two frightened lady friends to the safety of the cellar. A piece of shell passed right through her body and she expired almost immediately. Mr Merryweather was buried by debris inside the shop.

MEN OF YORKSHIRE
JOIN THE
NEW ARMY

And help to Avenge the Murder of innocent Women and Children in Scarborough, Hartlepool & Whitby.

Shew the Enemy that Yorkshire will exact a full penalty for this COWARDLY SLAUGHTER.

ENLIST TO-DAY

Recruiting Office:
ST. NICHOLAS STREET, SCARBOROUGH.

40 Broken plate glass windows at the premises of Charles Smith, the
antique dealer, in South Street. His premises were "greatly damaged" and much of his stock destroyed. Across the road, an em-
ployee of Clare & Hunt's, the chemists, was killed at the door, as
was a Mr Harry Frith who worked at W C Land & Co.

41 Picture by Professor Hoeger of 'The Panic at Scarborough' and
which was painted to commemorate the bombardment.

THE LAST OF THE LIGHTHOUSE, SCARBOROUGH BOMBARDMENT

42 Severe damage to Scarborough's lighthouse was caused by a shell which 'clipped' the side of the tower and, ricocheted and hit the end of the Grand Hotel. This postcard shows the dismantling of the damaged lighthouse after the raid.

43 In the period after the raid much damage was caused to shipping by the mines laid by the Kolberg. Minesweeper No. 58 was run ashore at Scarbrorough after hitting a mine off the town.

MINE SWEEPER No.58. DAMAGED BY GERMAN MINES OFF SCARBOROUGH.

44 Devastation at Whitby. The ancient ruins of Whitby Abbey, as well as local homes, were blasted by the German gunners.

45 Funeral cortege of the victims of the attack makes its way through the streets of Scarborough, December 20 1914. At the inquest on some of the victims of the bombardment the jury asked if it could return a verdict of wilful murder but the coroner advised that this would be futile as he would be thereby required to bind some person or persons over on the murder charge.

47 Opposite: Headline in *The Scarborough Pictorial*, December 23 1914.

TYNEMOUTH
South Shields
SUNDERLAND

HARTLEPOOL
Docks
WEST HARTLEPOOL
Seaton Carew Shelled
Tees Mouth
REDCAR
SALTBURN
MIDDLESBROUGH

Bombarded from 8.15 to 8.50 a.m. by 2 Battle CRUISERS & I Armoured CRUISER Estimated about 500 Shells fired 91 Killed including 30 WOMEN & 15 CHILDREN about 300 Wounded; Gasometer, Waterworks & Towns much damaged

WHITBY to HARTLEPOOL 28 Miles

HELIGOLAND NAVAL BASE to HARTLEPOOL 330 Nautical Miles or about 14 HOURS PASSAGE for a FAST CRUISER SQUADRON at 22-25 Knots their average speed; the journey can therefore be done under cover of NIGHT.

WHITBY Bombarded 9.15 to about 9.30 a.m. by 2 Battle CRUISERS, about 30 shells fired; 2 Men killed, 2 Boys wounded; Coastguard Sta. ABBEY, Town & inland villages damaged

St Hilda's Church
WHITBY
The ABBEY Shelled
RUSWARP Shelled
EAST CLIFF
River Esk

Eylingdale Moor

ROBIN HOOD'S BAY

RAVENSCAR

Petard Point

SCALBY

NORTH BAY
OLD CASTLE Shelled
OLD CASTLE WALLS Damaged
St MARY'S CHURCH Hit

SHOP Set on FIRE
BALMORAL HOTEL Hit
EASTBOROUGH
OLD HARBOUR
NEW HARBOUR
LIGHTHOUSE Damaged
MANY HOUSES HIT in this crowded quarter

PROSPECT ROAD
HOUSES Hit
GLADSTONE ROAD
HANOVER ROAD
HOUSES Hit
VICTORIA ROAD
HIGH ROAD
HOUSES Hit
WESTBOROUGH
BARWICK ST.
HOUSE Hit
CRESCENT
RAILWAY STA.
TOWN HALL
CAFÉ Struck
ROYAL HOTEL Hit
SOUTH BAY

ALGRAVE ROAD
WESTBORO' ROAD

GRAND HOTEL Struck 3 times

SCARBOROUGH
Bombarded from 8.5 to 8.25 a.m. by Battle CRUISER & Armoured CRUISER, estimated about 300 Shells fired; 17 KILLED including 8 WOMEN & 4 CHILDREN about 100 Wounded

RAMSDALE
PARK
VALLEY
ROAD
St MARTIN'S CH. Damaged

SOUTH CLIFF Shelled
PRINCE of WALES Hotel Hit

J.F. MORRELL.

Scarboro' Under Fire

MERCILESS DESCENT OF DEATH AND DESTRUCTION.

Defenceless Town Sacrificed to German "Kultur."

FUSILLADE OF 500 SHELLS.

Men, Women, and Children Killed.

WHOLESALE SHATTERING OF PROPERTY.

Many Miraculous Escapes.

"Since the raid the "lighting of shops at night order" is still more stringent; there are whole streets in which there is hardly a whole window pane, and hardly a street in which there is not some damage by shell or shrapnel splinters, although by now a lot is boarded up.

I should think quite half the people on the South Cliff have left the town, and Christmas trade is at a standstill.

On Thursday there was a great influx of sightseers into the town, and we also had some 2000 men of the Leeds Rifles brought here with 2 machine guns and an armoured car. I am also told that some heavy guns- howitzer type - were also brought here.

On Saturday all the shops closed from 11.45 to 1.15; and from 12.0 - 1.0 the Archbishop of York conducted a memorial service at St. Mary's; as luck would have it a customer or two who thought it silly and absurd of us to close, because they wanted goods, kept me at the shop till 12.20, and consequently I only saw the folks coming away from the service. I saw one of the funerals however. The members of the Wykeham Street family. Father (one of Cooper's R.F.A. men), wife, child and another infant, were all in one procession. Two hearses side by side for the seniors, the man's with a military bearing party and then behind an open landau with the two little coffins, followed by a company of soldiers with their officers.

We are protected nightly now by several warships in the bay, and we hear the Germans left any number of mines in and near the bay so there are a dozen or so mine-sweepers about. We heard later on Saturday that one of these had been blown up, and the crew landed here. During Meeting this morning, at which Maurice Rowntree and George Rowntree were fine, we heard a "special edition" being yelled out. On leaving Meeting we heard another mine-sweeper had gone and some of the survivors were being landed: so we tore down to the beach. The lifeboat was just in and the wounded and dead being taken up to various hospitals; we heard that there is some chance that they may get the boat towed in and save her.

We then wandered on to the harbour and there was the mine-swee- per that was blown up on Saturday with a hole under her bows big enough to drive a horse and cart through! She'd been towed in stern first, but how they managed to save her I don't know.

There is a shell hole right through the lighthouse and it has to come down, as it's most unsafe. We next journeyed on to the Marine Drive. A shell has struck the steps in front of the Cafe, gone on underneath the floor, apparently hit against rock and come up into the ladies' lavatory at the Cafe. It isn't half in a mess! Luckily we are tenants, not owners, and our lease ran out this autumn !

No Rowntree house has been damaged, save a little glass at W. Rowntree & Sons furniture stores, and the rumour is already round that we are pro-German and had given particulars of the position of our houses etc. to them, and consequently have been saved !

More funerals of victims are passing here now.

Harold and I were just off for a walk when a doctor's car came round, stopped, and took Harold off as he was wanted for ambulance work; where, I don't know.

I've got two rather extra good photos and I've sold the copyright of these to E.T.W. Dennis & Sons Ltd. for P.P.c.'s ! "

48 Part of C J Taylor's vivid eye-witness account of the aftermath of the raid, typed out December 20 1914. "I've got two rather extra good photos and I've sold the copyright of these to E T W Dennis & Sons Ltd. for P.P.C.'s!" The photographic works of Dennis's in Bellevue Street were, in fact, seriously damaged but the business survived to make the most of the opportunity presented: they issu- ed dozens of postcards showing the effects of the bombardment and also two commemorative booklets.

49 This photograph of the damage at Wykeham Street was embel- lished by the artist's addition of child and doll to make an emotive recruiting poster.

50 Opposite: Proclamation posted in Hartlepool following the attack.

MEN OF BRITAIN !
WILL YOU STAND THIS ?

Nº 2 Wykeham Street, SCARBOROUGH, after the German bombardment on Dec! 16th. It was the Home of a Working Man. Four People were killed in this House including the Wife, aged 58, and Two Children, the youngest aged 5.

78 Women & Children were killed and 228 Women & Children were wounded by the German Raiders
ENLIST NOW

WOMEN OF SCARBRO'

HELP TO AVENGE

THE

SLAUGHTER

OF THE

Innocent Women and Children

of Scarborough by

Encouraging MEN

TO

ENLIST at ONCE

Recruiting Office, St. Nicholas Hall, Scarborough

52 Feed the Guns Week in Scarborough. Armoured field gun parked outside the Pavilion Hotel at the very end of the War, November 11-16 1918. Memories of the attack are plainly still very much in mind.

53 Revenge ! One of the attackers, the *Derfflinger*, sinks to the bottom of Scapa Flow, June 21 1919.

HE GUNS.

SCARBOR'O.

he Guns, Scarborough Nov 17th to 19th '15
Designed by Tom Mellor

"Derffhinger's" last stage

54 An artist's impression of the effects of the bombardment of West Hartlepool. A shell passed right through the Baptist Chapel and rebounded into the bedroom of a house, killing a woman inside. A Territorial, going to her assistance, **had** his rifle blown from his hand. Local people are seen rushing **from** their homes to assist.

55 A picture aboard the *Derfflinger* based **up**on a sketch by a German naval officer who took part in the bombardment. As the *Daily Sketch* observed, "German Kultur means shells on churches."